GW01458978

When auntie was a crow

Jo Haslam studied Fine Art in Leicester and Manchester. She began writing poetry while bringing up her three children and working in community arts, in libraries and as a bibliotherapist in West Yorkshire where she and her partner still live. Her poems have appeared in magazines including *The Rialto, Ambit, Stand* and *PN Review* and have been placed in the National, Mslexia and Charles Causley poetry competitions. She has five collections, initially with Smith/Doorstop and subsequently with Templar Press after winning their Straid Collection Award in 2012.

When auntie was a crow

Jo Haslam

Pindrop Press

Published 2023 by
Pindrop Press
1 Oakwood Drive
Newton Mearns
Glasgow G77 5PU
UK

www.pindroppress.com

ISBN 978-1-7384059-1-6

A catalogue record for this book is available from the British Library.

Typeset by Pindrop Press (Palatino Linotype).

Acknowledgements

Acknowledgements are due to the editors of the following publications in which some of these poems first appeared: *Acumen, Ambit, Dreamcatcher, Grey Hen Press, Pennine Platform.*

A lyke wake for auntie was one of seven poems commended in the 2021 National Poetry Competition.

Deer on the Road won second prize in the Guernsey International Poetry Competition 2022.

The kiss won first prize in the Teignmouth Poetry Competition 2020.

When auntie was a crow won third prize in the Teignmouth Poetry Competition 2021.

Hide was commended in the York Poetry Prize 2021.

Vase of a hundred birds was shortlisted in the Wells Poetry Competition 2020.

The Language problem was shortlisted in the Bridport Poetry Prize 2020.

Working dog was longlisted in the Bridport Poetry Prize 2021.

For John who encouraged me and Auntie who gave me books

Contents

Notes on the Poems

When auntie was a crow

Crow auntie

She wasn't always a bird. Once, she was girl
long legged and slim, racing to school
on her bike. She didn't always speak
caw and *eark*. She knew Latin and Greek,
French irregular verbs. She didn't lurch
broken winged, shedding black feathers
over the floor. She wore pearls,
cashmere; her nails were red-glossed.
She didn't claw at the hospital blanket,
push back the tray of food; didn't sip
orange juice from a child's feeding cup;
she drank Calvados, Cointreau; didn't crave
rabbit or vole but *mille-feuille, champignons,*
omelette aux fines herbes. France was her thing.
She knew every stop on the metro. At night
the clack of her heels down its long corridors,
the whoosh of the doors as they opened –
Bastille, Pont Neuf, Lamarck - Caulaincourt.

Message

The answer phone says, *You have thirty- six*
new messages. We listen though we know
it's auntie every time. She rings the speaking clock,
neighbours, us every few minutes; sometimes
when we're with her, *Just checking*
she says, or, *I'm a bit confused,* or, *I rang you by mistake*
I do apologise. She has our number off by heart
but doesn't know when it's mealtimes, midnight,
half three in the morning. She doesn't go to bed,
doesn't pull the curtains closed, doesn't eat
the sandwiches the carer left unless we remind her.
Even then she doesn't eat them. When she's not on the phone
she wanders through the quiet house or sleeps
in the chair, chin sunk to her chest, starts awake
to realise Bill's no longer there. I listen to her voice
plaintive, reproachful, the voice of an abandoned child.
I show her the phone bill: *Look,* I say, *how many times*
you've rung, but she denies it. *I know the time*
she says, *I can count,* and count she does, the months,
weeks, days; backwards from twenty for the doctor.

A lyke wake for auntie

By Asda, Tesco, Boggart Hole,
its river path and bowling green;
by midweek cold and dank October,
by the Co-Op funeral parlour

by paramedic, ambulance,
by CT scan and mammogram,
by all night on the floor alone,
by fire *that burns to the bare bone*

no one kept her company
till she *from hence away*
had passed, nobody stayed
for *the ae neet* and no one lit

a candle in the dark.
No one stayed *by fire or fleet*
and no one stayed her soul to keep;
but some came early, some were late

some took the wrong exit
on the motorway. And nobody
remembered much of anything
she'd said or done. No one wept.

Some didn't come. Nobody knew
what job she'd done, name of the caff
where every day she ate her lunch;
no one followed her on foot

no one took the river path,
but someone chucked the pee
stained mat, cleared the wardrobe
packed her clothes, gave what they'd take

to Oxfam, Hospice, Age UK.
And someone tucked her wedding ring
and glasses case inside the box,
someone touched her freezing hands

17

and someone prayed, by Asda, Tesco,
Boggart Hole, by fire that burns
to the bare bone, by Lethe, Styx
and Irwell, *Christ receive her saule.*

When auntie was a crow

You could hear her the length of the hospital ward,
the rasped *aarrk aark aark* she couldn't stop
so the woman in the next bed clapped on her headphones,
the manager come from the care home said *no,*
as they all did; and no wonder: who could sleep
through all that cawing, who'd want a crow
or jackdaw to feed, put to bed,
who'd want to lift the cumbersome body,
sweep up the shed feathers, chance the claws
and fierce beak. And what will you feed her
when everything's pushed away? What she needs
is relief, some quiet to soothe her, some food
she can eat; a mole or skinned squirrel,
peanuts or ants; and some place to fly from.
And she'd fly if she could, if she hadn't fallen,
rolled on the floor in the night flailing and calling
unable to shift her dense bones; if her unwieldy limbs
weren't caught in the cellular blanket; if
she had a branch to perch on, black-winged, ready
to lift into the dazzle of sky and no weight at all.

The speaking tube

Your mother has taken the tube from her throat
and left it to soak overnight in a glass of water.
The metal still holds her fingerprints,
the glass is filmed with her breath.
When she touches the hole at her neck
her voice is released as a hiss
or croak. It's a struggle to put the tube in
and sometimes she can't be bothered.
Her speaking tube, she says, as if her voice
had a life of its own, as if it might whistle
or break into song, as if it might wake in the night
and call to her – Annie, Annie –
and she'd have to hush it quiet.
But now she mouths the words, as she did in the mill
when she couldn't be heard over the clack
of the looms; when she longed to be out
on the moor, when her voice could carry
over the wind and blown grass, when she could call
to her sister, her friends, when she could sing,
Barb'ry Allen, Molly Malone, Annie Laurie.

Long house

Our houses, docked in the valley
anchored in billows of peat moor
and clough; built slant, so no surface
meets at a right angle. We walk with a roll
across the tipped floor, a buffer
of wood behind the skirting to keep
the line straight. When we cut the doorway
between hall and kitchen, stone
filled the skip. White dust leached through
emulsion and plaster held sea-washed husks
of fossils and shells. Broken clay pipes
bleach under the flags. Despite its squat weight
no foundations to speak of. We plug
holes and patch, but moss felts the windows,
rain drives under the slates. At night
we cast off, blown in the dark, mid-ocean,
with only our freight of snails and toads, mice
in the roof space, swallows come back
to nest in the eaves startled into flight.

Signs

Now they're old men, my brother
and his friends, they don't go out much,
my brother not even to Deaf Club.
His legs aren't steady since the stroke.
Glaucoma's done for his right eye.
He can't see bus numbers, might stumble
in the road, won't sense someone
stealing close behind. They sit together,
Peter, Frank and Samuel, list on their hands
which friends gave in to illness, lost their wives.
They're slower now so we can follow, and each year
fewer names. But when I was a girl
how they'd crowd through the door, flushed
and beer-breathed. For all they couldn't hear
the world teemed in them. Crammed in
our narrow kitchen their hands flew like birds.

Working dog

In the wholefood shop we stop to stroke
a dog called Luna. Her nose pushed in our hands
is cold and velvet soft. She's like the one
your father had, a quick smooth coated greyhound
who'd race with you across the moor; a dog
you carried three miles home, foam bubbling
at her mouth; the one I mix up
with our own long-gone border cross.
And I say ours but mean our son's
who'd whistle him over another moor,
a dog who'd run all day and night if he could,
who cleaved to him when everything was wrong;
a dog who haunted us. We'd wake
thinking we heard the click of his claws
or his dream-troubled whine,
this dog who is both he and she, our son's
but also yours and mine, your father's
and this poem's; rough-coated and smooth-furred,
moon-shone, black and white, a long muzzled
gentle hound – you'd never say *beloved*
of a dog, never *soul* though it grieves
for him the most; never say *mourn* or *yearn*
but know one day he'll come, quick,
sure-footed, spun from light and air;
the miles he'll run, tireless and weightless
across cold grass and mud; for rabbit,
stoat, fox musk; for ball or stick or home.

Offering

A gift to the water god, my pen
in the grating of the *Plaça Reial;*
the pen I'd just found after months.
I'd fumed at its loss, mourned it almost
as if the words I might write
with it had also gone. I thought of the case
breaking up, ink-leak in the water,
saw the words blur, dissolve on the page;
but lost anyway, my poems
on yellowing paper, gathering dust or dumped
in a bin by a heedless son or daughter.
And what could I say that the water
doesn't each day as it trickles through gutters
and culverts; and not so far away,
the sea heaving itself on and back
from the shore. And here is the rain
dousing the heat of the city, washing it grey
then gleaming it coloured again.

The language problem

We write your address in English
and Chinese, hope the thing arrives.
In English we start with your name,
end with the place you live, and the space
around you widens. In Chinese,
other way round, and we end focused on you
six thousand miles away. We study the two
as if they were a puzzle and you the solution hidden
in-between like the illusion that intrigued us as children
where a face becomes a candlestick. But this is language
and brings us up against your escape
into another life, sleeping in your small hot room
while we wake to rain against the window,
lupins flattened in the garden. You call
to say it's midnight and still forty degrees,
you can't sleep. *Read something*
I say, although you've left behind most of your books.
I keep them with your drawings, cards, your shoes
and winter coat, jumpers folded in the drawer.
All this, not so much a puzzle
as a need; yours to go and mine
to have you close. Halfway across the world
your voice rises and fades. I switch to loudspeaker
and you're here again. With the phone it's easy,
the familiar exchange; requests for notebooks,
paints; you making headway with Chinese,
how I'm defeated by it; and unsaid
the things I can't put in the letters
I don't write, though if I could I'd write to you
in all the world's languages. Instead,
this parcel with posters, magazines, my scribbled note,
address it's taken hours to get right;
how long, you ask, *until it's here*, and I don't know.
But sooner or later everything arrives, letter
to its destination, traveller to the place
they dreamed of, this package with its tokens
of your former life at your door,
ink blurred, paper torn and stained. Be careful
when you open it, there's rain inside; patches of grey sky.

By hand

after wood engraver Thomas Bewick who made many of his own engraving tools

By candlelight; by craft.
By peering close at how the feathers lie.
By bone.
By tense and slide of muscle
under fur. By burin, graver,
spitsticker. By making his own.
By knowing when they're sharp
enough. By stone.
By hand in sync with eye.
By practice.
By stipple, hatch and line.
By grain of bark; by branch.
By bird and beast and leaf. By cloud
and windblown grass. By bringing light
from dark. By years
of wearing out his eyes,
this print no bigger than his palm.

Deer on the road

Out of the mist, on the road for home, he veered past our car;
and no signs anywhere, though those trees higher up
are called Hartwood. And though he was gone so suddenly,
he won't disappear; the dark solidness and startled eyes.
When I close my own he floats in front like that Ice Age deer
in the flow of the river, or the hart of dreams, but real,
earth-coloured. And I don't know why we didn't stop and
follow him
over sodden fields, through clinging drops of mizzle,
wavering things catching our feet, damp hair snagged
by twigs and leaves; till we reach the copse on the slope
of the hill, where we're the dream, soaked and unsure
why we've come this far with nothing in sight,
but unable to leave the deep night of the woods
till he leaps in front, the star of his rump glimmering white.

Swifts

What are these birds but a clinker of bone,
a handful of feathers and dust; seeds sown
on the wind, their fast beating hearts
geared for flight. They are small boats

out at sea that veer with the swing
of tides. They have heard whales sing,
flown miles above cloud, past aeons of ice;
have seen the dark lift; that sudden light

at the rim of the earth. All this
and no more weight than a dried leaf.
What else can they do but trust
in the instinct that tingles the spine?

And they have the drum of their hearts
to steer by. *Go,* say these hearts and they rise.

Owl (1)

Oh months they've been gone
but one trembled call
and we know they're back
lifting the hood of the night
in the woods. How the leaves
quake and sigh,
as we do, awake in the dark.
Like, calling to like –
the peewits' sore cry on the moor,
seabirds that mourn on the shore.

Owl (2)

Call him *Hoolet, Billy Wix* come back to haunt
this rise of stone and brick where woods should be;

see him drift, soundless through the few trees left
beak primed to spear the prey that slips

beneath this floor of twig and leaf. And here's his *whoo
tu whit,* the white disc of his face, head

that twists three-quarters clockwise, torch-beam eye
that spans the orbit of his loss:

churchyard, field, ghost trunks
of ash and beech; *Billy Wix,* his choke

of gristle, bones and teeth, his clockwise
fright, his core's white twist,

his torch-beam screech, his blind
ninety degrees, his heart's midnight.

Blackbird

Who makes each night from our low roof his rapt
disclosure to the sky and through our open window.
Each season a new song; he'll practise till he gets it right.
Listen how it comes and goes through house and garden, woods,
the hills beyond. At each pause we wait
as if our lives depended on it. And if I said *flute*
or *pure,* it wouldn't mean a thing. But come
into the evening quiet; he's perched as high
as our roof will allow, his beak is open, lifted up,
its yellow deep as the sky is fathomless,
his note cool as its far-off blue,
as clear as this unclouded moon
that comes up pale and new, as single as its silver rim,
as round as any coin you'd take into your mouth to test.

New

This rain has taken the leaf
back to its beginning
back to its new green,
each drop on the surface
curved as an ear, tuned to its own
sibilant tongue, as an eye
cleared to see its colour repeat
down the valley, tree after tree.

Outbreak

He shows me his rash; faint pink blotches
under the skin. I have to look close
to see anything. Then there's the ingrown hair
and the pus-filled pimple he wants me to lance.
I hold a needle in the gas flame
till it glows red, before I perform
the primitive surgery. He tells me about his stomach
condition; how it started and when. How he won't ever eat
mushrooms again. He's convinced
he's got threadworms and I have to check.
I haven't done this since he was a baby.
And he's got medicine; creams for the rash,
bottles of stuff for his stomach,
tablets for worms. As for his heart,
I search the cupboards for the sealed blister
packs to heal his brokenness.

Bending the spoons

Remember how watching that man who bent
the forks we thought it all a trick?
That was till we saw the metal
shift under your hands like liquid.
Look, you said, and we did
as the spoon you stroked curved back
across your fingers.

Then there were my knitting needles
that whizzed round in your fists.
Something to do with heat and magnetism,
the way you know your way home without a map
or directions, your nose for a dodgy deal,
that instinct for what's true,
how dogs come to you, how you touch
the strings of your guitar and coax
them into music. And there's the way you held

on to our son when we'd almost lost hope
he'd find himself, how you ran
with him into the wind along a shingle beach,
the sun going down and the sea turned to pewter,
how that wind whipped through his hair
and stung his cheeks to colour.

The blessing

A blessing on our granddaughter
in her pink cushioned car seat
bought for us by her mother.
A blessing on the motorway to Manchester
the highest in England. A blessing
on its seven miles of rain and wind-scoured moor
that take us into Lancashire.
A blessing on our granddaughter
come with us to meet her English cousins
three of whom she hasn't seen.
A blessing on the road to Rivington
(its green fields, hill known as *Pike*)
that brings us to their door. A blessing on the motorway
chock full of Fords, Toyotas, Astras, delivery vans
and wagons; their nose to tail of exhausts,
bumpers, headlights haloed in misty vapour.
A blessing on our granddaughter
in her *Dora the Explorer* raincoat, wellies,
hand-knitted mittens threaded through her jumper;
on her name which means *flower*
in her father's language. A blessing on her all the way
to Lancashire. A blessing on the water
slanted on our windscreen.
A blessing on the water seeping through the peat bog.
A blessing on the water black and secret in March Haigh,
the reservoir we walked to yesterday.
 A blessing on the mist wreathed round our Nissan Micra.
A blessing on our granddaughter
the spit of her father.
A blessing on her only words
of Arabic; her father not the best
of teachers. A blessing on her *shukran, anhaar,*
binti, la. A blessing on our granddaughter
woken to the world six years ago.
A blessing on our granddaughter born late
to her mother. A blessing on our granddaughter.
Every day a blessing on her.

Alone

Your mother rings me early morning,
says you won't sleep alone,
you've been disturbed by too much noise
too many visitors. I hear you crying down the phone.

Your rage fills the world of your four walls.
Your mother's had to hold you the whole night.
You don't know you're no longer linked.
The sea sounding in her ears is all
her blood and heat but she'll wake to your cry
however much she craves her separate sleep

and however much the world expands to take you in
she'll feel, as I do years and miles away, the echo
of its shock waves in her bones , like whales
who sing their kin round the circumference of the globe.

At Lovell Quinta

When we get there at last, it's just us
and two dog walkers; the ringing silence
of the woods. We've come to see the Swamp Cypress
and Red-Twigged Lime, his sixty-five species

of ash. Odd this passion in a man so focussed
on the heavens but perhaps he wanted certainty.
And what more fixed than a tree, its rootedness,
its solid girth. And if he never planted one

we still think of him bent-backed, palms creased
with dirt, nails moon-rimmed in black.
With planting you have to get close to the earth,
tune to its deep workings, how one thing roots

one fails, another scatters. As for these galaxies
of leaf and branch and what they sing,
mysterious as any cloud of dust or gas:
ash keys in the wind, sudden rain of beechmast.

The vase of a hundred birds

They could have been crows
sheering up from the fields,
peewits coursing the winter sky,
swans with necks entwined;
but more likely cranes, in a repeat
with petal and leaf; though the only one
we saw that day was the blackbird,
through the high window of the museum
dipping his beak to a pool of clear water.
How the drops arced and gleamed.
I thought of the hands of the potter
round the cool clay spinning his crane into flight,
light bones and keeled sternum yearning
for sky; how each bird curves
in its own way; dove from the sleeve
and dove come back; that one set free
by Matisse from a sheet of blue paper
then a new one released with each turn
of the wrist till they're numberless,
till they're one curve and one bird,
plover and chaffinch, dunnock
and swift, the blackbird, his yolk-yellow beak.

Home boy!

The way his bulk moved, that resigned flop
and sigh. How his basket creaked, the snort
before he'd settle, the dreaming scrabble
 of his paws. Six months. And when I come inside
out of a windblown rainy night he still slips past me
at the door; that smell of leaf mould
oil and mud, nudge of his rough coat
against my leg, thump of his tail and shove
of his nose in my palm. I almost bend
to press my cheek against his pricked ear
to put an arm around his damp cold fur
and hear what I still hear, his whimper
and bark, his belch, which is thanks for the food
or his soul as it moves through gut and bowel.

My brother tells me his heart

He makes a snapping motion with his fist
then thumps it against his side.
This means his heart is broken.
He tells me he's in bed now every night
by nine; signs the double lock for door,
shivers and hugs himself to show
how frightened he is *when he forgets.*
This is since he lost his wife.
He says he dreams she touches him,
his shoulder, cheek, the place
he thinks his heart is, head. And I have them
now in mine, the broken and the pulsing.
Sometimes he says he cries a little,
shows me an inch of space
between his forefinger and thumb.
How can you measure grief? What can I say?
Go inside, its cold, make sure you lock the door.
I indicate the turning of a key.

Fingula

I dreamed myself swan on black cold water,
mouth stunned to gold,
webbed feet a strangeness. I sleep
out of the ken of other birds.

I dreamed myself maiden; the face
I dip into the lough, haunted
by her eyes' round shock. Nine hundred
years not long enough to speak the loss
if there were words, and words were mine
to call my brothers home .

I dreamed myself bird given grace
to sing; but if it's to be heard,
the sound that shapes the song must burn
along the bone and thrill the wing.
I turn, and listen for an echo
on the water, *Fiachra, Aod, Con.*

Fiachra

The surprise was the weight.
That and the pain, small prickles
under the skin, then a raised rash –
we thought some childhood thing
though shoulder blade was an odd place
to start. Next was the down,
velvet as moss over stone.
We rubbed the cream in
for each other, felt the hard nubs
jutting through the skin.

We kept wanting to slip out of bed,
drawn to the window, clouds speeding across
the night sky. The owl spoke to us,
the grey geese headed south. We opened
our mouths to reply but no sound
came out. We couldn't sleep
anymore on our backs. We left
our nightclothes by the window,
four heaps of white like shed feathers.
Aoife offered a gift and we begged,
If one thing's to stay let it be music.
We never thought it would be wings.

Margana

Night is never silent here. Listen
how the pylons thrill their electric messages.
Their strung song has you alert,
each thrum and click tuned to the strike
of a clock you can't alter or divert.

And there's the owl that weeps
through the woods; his low *shrik, shrik*
plucks your nerves. You know his beak
and talons, the sweep and curve
of his orbit, how his head turns
through the full circle of your sleep

while those creatures still awake, that steal
through the undergrowth, come
to your attention. Their least rustle
in the dark is magnified. As for the moon
remote and lemon pale; it has a thin song
of its own but too far away
to hear. The hare knows it though: see
how he leaps, a meteor under its light.

New moon

is an eye
just opening, sleep-dazed,
on its side. *What*
what are these drifts
and obscurations, these pinpricks
of light? It can't cope.
Let it sleep, disconsolate,
listing. Let it bide.
Let it grow
rounder and bolder each night.

Hare

The hare in his form,
still as if his breath had gone,
his blood didn't run,
his skull was stone,
as if he'd never
raced or leapt – until he does
then his breath is fire
his blood quicksilver
his skull opens like a flower.

Solstice

Owl on the edge of the dark, calling his woe;
fox sunk, ribbed with hunger; mole at his labour
alone in his sightless earth. Famine month,
the cold of the world and the loss of light –
oh bring us the moon, its one good eye,
bring us the night stung with stars;
bring us the sun blood-red in the morning sky.

Impassable terrain

You text us in the middle of the night
from somewhere in the mountains.
You've forgotten we're six hours behind
and I don't say. You tell us your next destination
but we've checked the route already;
rockfalls, passes blocked, weather closing in.
You'll make the journey anyway
impelled by a need I can't identify.
Son, I want to ask, *what are you searching for?*
But perhaps you don't know, although some god
somewhere may have the answer.
But we don't believe in gods, do we? Demons
are another matter; the ones that left you raging,
then for months hopeless and afraid;
our footloose boy with no good ground
beneath him. Even then, snow pale
and strained, your impulse was to *go*.
And now they're in your sights;
improbable blue peaks, a sky so cold
and bright it hurts to look. So I don't tell you
how our own is creeping grey, how mild our July,
its few days of heat and how tonight it rained.
I can hear it through the open window
falling on the garden, and now I've lost
the thread of sleep. I don't tell you this either,
or how I've planted sweet peas, tended them
like children, and they've flowered, pink,
deep plum and white, reaching skywards
through the trellis. They smell like honey.
And I'm glad of the rain, its quiet fall,
still cool when I go out. I say none
of this, trust you to keep your own
good sense, your father's instinct
for direction. And I wish you heat, rain
when you need it; honey. I wish
you godspeed. I wish you blue mountains.

The stone head

Our stone Buddha head left in the garden
all summer is covered in moss
and verdigris. I bring it inside
to soap it clean then take a soft brush
to the tilted lips and long, lidded eyes.
When I'm done the stone is tinged pink.
For a minute I'm shocked, as if some magic
has taken place, though it's not even stone
just moulded concrete and four ninety-nine
from the cut price shop. Reason says
something odd in the mix, but when I'm outside
I keep touching the face for something
like heat, for a flush on the cheeks
like the rose blush of sky in the east.

Twenty moons

for Modwenna

We all said the same thing, *bad news;*
her best friend can't believe she won't
just walk through the door. And those of us
who thought she still breathed, who thought
she almost stirred; but it was just a gust of air
through the open window, lifting the chequered scarf
around her neck, her dark red hair;
I noticed how the heavy velvet curtain moved.
And still we can't believe the sea-sound
of her womb is hushed, her flamy hair won't reignite:
how could its hundred thousand fires be doused,
and those hands, their fifty-four small separate bones
reduce to ashy dust, or any night swallow up
their twenty moons when no dark is dark enough?

Under the hill

after Wendell Berry

To know the dark, go blind
into this three-mile tunnel,

lie on your back and push
with all the force you have.

Just the one way
through the hill. Take no

caged bird or lamp.
You're under the earth.

Know its deep time, its caves
of ice, its seabed

sediment. Be acquainted
with your dead. Understand

your heart is opening. The lamp
you didn't have will shine

the bird will sing. Your heart
will beat its own dark wings.

Snow

has fallen
come in the night
sudden and silent
and the world
for the moment
is clean and unspoken

snow has fallen
nothing so lovely
so cold and so white
nothing so bright
not moonlight or starlight

Anemones

Not from the sky
these stars at our feet
but white gleamed
anemones
under the trees.

Fox

Not much in the way of pickings tonight
for the fox in the cold, on the highway,
the field; sliding under the five-barred gate,
skirting the path at the back of the house.

Her brush is down, her tongue hangs out.
The sky is shot with a fire of frost;
the dustbins are sealed with a rim of ice.
By morning that ice has set to stone

and hunger is locked in her heart and bones.
The chicken coop is bolted and dark;
skip emptied at the back of the pub.
But she noses for scraps, snouts for leavings

strews the contents of black bin bags
over the tarmac: potato peelings
banana skins, smashed eggshells and carrot tops,
salami slice from a pizza box.

Her world spins its fire of frost. She pads
its ground's diamond crust, ears alert for stoat
or mouse while in their earth her cubs
two copper brooches sleep, curled head to foot.

Odd wombs

I imagine them laid end to end
bumping each other or rocked
like that toy, weighted to bob from side
to side when pushed, our odd wombs
in a line, my mother's, grandmother's
mine and my daughter's, none able
to bring a child out the right way. And the child
in each of them curled nose to knee
or pressed head to toe, our *Franks*
our *Extended Breeches*, our *Footlings*
coming out blind; our daughter blue as a damson
till the air was pushed into her lungs;
for days the L-shape of her under the blanket:
years ago chances were she'd have died.
Now with her own, she's booked in
for the cut. The oracle midwife
palpates the bump for a buttock or foot,
lays her hands flat on the swollen belly
and the day is named for her odd womb
to give up its new life out of the mess
of mucus and blood. And it's all the same
the waiting and terror, the body
in flood, till here she is
stunned with the child in her arms.

Breath

When they held her up, our newborn
daughter, bruised and blue,
and cleared the mucus from her mouth and pushed
the breath into her lungs
and I heard her first seagull cry
I thought of the keel-hauled sailor, forced to plunge
the water's dark and cold,
heaved to the surface gasping
and on his face the air's huge benediction.

Breech

Your baby's not turned. At thirty-six weeks
her head is still wedged near your heart.
You can feel the hard butt of it under your arm
when you shift in the night. She'll come out
feet-first if she gets the chance.
Let's hope they're intact, eyes and ears
her nose and mouth you saw on the scan
open and close as she swims
through your murmuring dark. Little fish, little bird
when she's propelled or tugged clear

feet flexed to start her miraculous progress
the soreness she's left will be layered
deep in the ache of your bones.
For the moment, here is her head
on your shoulder, your breast,

flopped on your neck or settled
in the crook of your elbow. And here she is
turning and turning again into the wide
blue of the world, little bird, little fish –
you haven't begun to miss her yet.

Shower in August

The Perseids, little flecks of dust
we call meteors or shooting stars
burn up once a year, the hottest month,
month of your birth.

Those days of freakish heat, the landscape
luminous at dusk – nights I walked
restless – if Perseids streaked the sky
they went unnoticed. We counted

off the days as we moved deeper into August.
From now the year declines, but tonight
In the cooling air the stars blaze;

these summer months that by accident
or fate, you've taken as yours; August when
the Perseid showers come, radiant, sudden as love.

White tulips

Let us speak about the tulips,
white with a hint of yellow,
the way their petals are both silky and tough.

Let us speak of how those petals close
and the small round heads are balanced
on grey- green stems. How we'd forgotten

we'd planted them. How they pushed up
in cold March days. How they flowered
in April. How they fade and fall

extravagantly, shedding petals in deep piles
on the path. How we take delight
in such excess. How one broke

and was rescued, held together
with sticky tape and stands now in a glass vase
on the table. How we can see

the yellow veins spread through the white.
How it's the first thing we look at
in the morning and the last at night.

Tagetes

I've left them to flourish as they should,
long leaves and woody stems,
the pinwheel heads of scarlet, bronze
and saffron. They smell of musk

and pepper; of apothecary cupboards
stored with cloves and cinnamon:
Flor de Muerto. In Mexico
they pave the way for dead souls

to return. I pick off a spent head
and split the fluted chalice to reveal
its dreaming regiment of seeds.
Disturbed in their wintering

each fletched black quill
quivers like an eyelid in the depth of sleep.

Dandelion

It lodges between paving stones,
pokes through cracks in concrete
gardens. *puff-ball, yellow-gowan.*

It flourished in the urban parks
where we'd count its blown parachutes.
clock-head, pissenlit, weed.

The Chinese revere its bitter root,
a cure for eczema, toothache, melancholy.
Pu gong ying. It tastes of earth and childhood

medicines. We loved its dark cordial
the best. In those aimless summers
in city parks that smelled of grass

and dust, we had no need of remedies.
We didn't know what time it was.

The possible weather

is on the next page of the Hiroshige
calendar we sent to our son
when he was caught
in his mind's net; when he was lost
to himself: this gift
of a high yellow sky, chrysanthemum,
blue serene water, blown petals
of cherry and plum
which will blossom next year
when the snow has gone.

Tree

As much as it's root which is tap,
it is blind reach through loam –
it is search for moisture, anchor
and home – as much as it's trunk
it is woody and vascular
tissue – it is quest for light, it is time
in circular mode – it is sap
and heartwood, dry bark
and resinous, peeled in strips
or flakes – it is branch
spread sideways and above, alone
or neighbourly – it is leaf
palmate and pinnate, entire
or serrated – it is tongues
whispering, it is rustle and stir
it is beech and ash
alder and birch – it is willow
bending to water.

Snail

In drip and slick, in teeming rain
snail in his spiral
shell of yellow
black and green, uncurls
and lifts antennae, turns
this way, that, alert
to his glue-gleam slime
trail, snake-path mazed
across our flags. Oh desert tracts
oh continents
to inch
across, oh gastropod
be not unnerved by distance
or ascent, observe
your kin achieve his vertical
see how he climbs
and clings
to our bedroom window.

The clocks

Neither of your clocks are working,
but then they're from the junk shop
so what can you expect?

You bought them for the polished wood,
brass fittings on the sides; art deco
inlay on the smaller, chimes

that strike each quarter hour.
Now both of them have stopped at three
as If they had one mind, or time,

or no time, although you'd say
there's only time and time – my brother's
which drags minute by excruciating minute

in his quiet house; our son's
halfway across the world and half
a day in front; our own, too fast, behind,

never enough; and that time in the night
when you're awake, the only sound
the loud tick tock. At least your clocks

are silent. But now you want them running;
wind and move them to a warmer place,
ease the casings off, adjust the wheels

and cogs. But these two are having none
of it. I scrutinise the frozen face
of this one on the landing. It tells me time

is circular and not the headlong train
I thought it was. When I jog it by accident
it strikes, a spectral sound that echoes

round the house, but not for long.
I'm secretly relieved although I know

we can't escape our deadlines, in-trays,

to do lists, shrinking all the time
we've got. And we have other clocks;
cheap alarm, the speaking, radio and phone,

the one whose glass has broken off – fair game
for our granddaughter who spins the fingers
round and on, then spins them back again.

Waterways

 A river is just rain and melted ice
and given that it rains enough
any one forced underground
can rise; this stream for instance, lost
below Tib Lane, bubbled into cellars
to nonplus bartenders and shopkeepers;
the Medlock skulking into culverts
below Oxford Road, snaking up
at Gaythorn. And others we thought disappeared
forever leave their trace
at Withy Grove and Upper Brook.

A river's names are various
but mostly they mean water:
Tamar, Tame and Rush, the Ouse and Wye.
Below ground or above, they have one aim
in mind – Mersey heading for the Irish Sea,
Tiber to Tyrrhenian, Guadalquivir
singing its name four thousand
miles to the Atlantic.

And those that never fill again
leave their ocean memory in desert sands
billowed to waves, limestone caverns
shot with shells and coral, this brook
where our children practised Ducks and Drakes,
aspiring to dry land. But anything can bring it back –
a shift of wind, sudden squall of rain,
a young boy skimming pebbles from the bank.

The Moon Under Water

In the end we don't stop at the Moon
Under Water pub on Deansgate,
although we're hungry and beguiled
by its two meals, eight ninety-nine.
But I'm struck by the name
and as we reach Little Ancoats
that water's taken shape, fog-bound and chill
as in a Valette painting, secret as the rivers
that still seam the city underground –
the Tib that only comes back after rain,
the Irk thirty feet below Victoria Station.

And if its future gleams now, steel and glass,
the city's past still breathes at Mendel's, Watts
and Castlefield's – vast warehouses I thought I'd make
a poem from – but here I am; a girl clutching her hat
racing to school past Fountain Street, Spring Gardens,
the canal, and on by Birch and Platt,
Crowcroft , Belle Vue, Kirkmanshulme
till all the years I lived here are a step across
their buried waters; the poem I thought
I'd write replaced by this about a pub
where we didn't eat, rivers I've never seen
and those I knew, the Gore and Gort, the Rush;
Birch Brook as clear as it has ever been.

Irwell

I am the Irwell, let me speak

my history of mud and grief

in stagnant puddles, little trickles

underground. Let me mourn

my loss of weed and dragonfly

the silver gleam

of darting minnow, kestrel

hovering – let me sing

the blue-green flash

of kingfishers on Deerplay Moor

where I was new

and quick, my name *White Spring.*

Dene

Where's the Dene?

Underground for years now
not mentioned, mapped,
not brought to mind,
not missed, not seen;
who knows if it's ever been?

Where did it run?

Along Shudehill and Withy Grove,
a six-inch stream a man could wade
in stockinged feet; a woman cross
with skirts hitched up, despite the mud,
despite the muck, till at Hanging Ditch
the northern arch of Hanging Bridge,
its course was lost, if course it did.

Where has it gone?

Into the dark and still asleep
bedded down, where willows
grow in boggy ground.
A hidden seam. How can it breathe
when *mucke* and *fylthe* have stopped
its mouth, how can it wake
when only rain remembers it?

Medlock

Thirteen hours of teeming rain
river bank and bridges gone
earth and headstone, urn and cross
the Medlock washed us from our graves.
Storm and flood and coffin wood
bring us up by grace of God.

Separated kin from kin
ankle, shin and shoulder blade
some to float and some to drown
some to swim and some to save.
Storm and flood and coffin wood
leave us be by grace of God.

Break of sky and race of cloud
we were heaved from underground
some to splinter some to cleave
some struck dumb and some to speak:
storm and flood and coffin wood
pray the Lord our souls to keep

Some are broken some are whole
who will count us, who will know
pelvis, knuckle, rib and skull
will they match us bone to bone?
Storm and flood and coffin wood
come to light by grace of God.

Some will wake and some will sleep
some will pray their souls to keep
some will founder, some know peace
some will hunger for the sea.
Storm and flood and coffin wood
pray the Lord deliver us.

Cellar

Last night our neighbour's cellar filled with water.
He's baffled as to where it's from
but the man who lived there once, would tell us
how each winter this same cellar

was awash. He'd venture down its steps
clutched candle held aloft
to see a swirl of liquid inching up the walls.
We hazard hidden well or some offshoot

of the river just yards from our door.
Listen, I say, *how it pours over the weir,*
how it sounds in the night, a gale
in the trees or an engine thrumming.

But our neighbour's talking tests
and measurements, talking pumps
and gauges. And now they're here,
men in yellow jackets, wagons,

flashlights, water pumping steadily
across the flags. The cellar fills again
and they can't fathom it.
Best leave it to its own devices

this water come up from the dark.
See how it rises and sinks back
like those rivers of my childhood,
Irk and Dene, surfaced from below

the city streets, with their memories
of downpour, flood and seethe, their increments
of seep and trickle, of skies that weep,
their ubiquity of wet that infiltrates

the smallest chink or crack,
that bubbles up when least
expected. Witness our gutters leaked,
walls slicked black, damp patches

on the ceiling. And here's our neighbour
intent now on peeling back
the layers of his house, floorboards lifted,
plaster chipped from walls,

digging down through earth and roots
and leaves, until he's reached some liquid dark...
and far enough, I think, for these geographies
of loss and dream. So let's stop here

with that long-buried neighbour
on his cellar stair, the gust of air
that makes his candle quiver,
water running past him like a river.

Jade axe   4000- 2000 BC

Dreamed from its world of cloud and peaks,
polished for days to balance and sheen
it leans to water, veins threaded like hair
or weed; mists at a breath to an ocean
of rain; and no trace of earth, grass or wood,
no stain of blood or sweat on the keen edge
that hangs like a tear at the base.

Hide

Those creatures that turn white in snow –
mountain hare, stoat, arctic fox
pale as the ground he streaks across –
bring to mind others of their kin,
swans spelled from their human skin,
deer blanched to ghost by *leucism*. You'd follow him
into the hushed white middle of the wood
to see if he'd dissolve as hoar frost does when touched
but he's always a length in front, a shimmering dot
like Grimshaw's *Woman in the Snow,*
or your mother in the fractured light
of Granny's road – you miles behind on leaden feet –
although the story where she leaves is in the note
propped on the mantle shelf when you're fourteen.
Your poems sleep inside the dream whose deer's
a swan, mouth stretched to sing,
its broken leg a trailing wing that spills
four spots of dark blood on the frozen ground.
And swans will grieve their withered skin,
ghost deer bleed red as any living thing,
mother go but never leave; a woman
who one night slips on her winter coat,
white high heels, and taps out of the silent street
into your poem's ice and snow.

Em

My mother dead these twenty years
keeps coming back. By day
I hardly think of her but night
brings the dream I wake from sweating
and someone I can't see
calling her name – *Em, Emmie. Emily.*
She's turning down the lane
towards my grandma's house. I'm five
and can't keep up and when I reach
the corner where the hedge is thickest
she's so far ahead I think I'll never
catch her. I dream that I'm fifteen
and she's leaving forever. *Hush*
you say, *you're crying in your sleep.*
I want to push her back between her sisters
Ivy, Dot and Nell, into the past
she belongs in. I hold my hands to my face
as if I'd made a binding spell
but she still follows me; you'd think *she*
was the child, you'd think *I'd* abandoned *her.*
I can't escape. Daylight
and she's here again. She makes
my insides burn. She turns my skin to fire.

Em's version

Who wants the truth when all it does is hurt?
Who wants to see the heart cut in two?
Take note of everything I'm telling you.
Cold hands, they say, *warm heart.*

Well, my hands were burning, skin on fire
for another's touch. As for my heart,
it was a starved dog,
a rusted pail, a soiled dish cloth.

I made this up. My heart was a book
with nothing written in it.
That book is shut. I never read
a book that wasn't lies. I had to lie

to cut myself in two. I made this up.
And everything I'm telling you is true.

Caul (1)

Little helmet, membrane, hood,
translucent tissue, sailor's luck.

Little cobweb, second skin,
little fragile clinging thing.

Peel it off; now sink or swim.

Caul (2)

Just one more superstition to go with all the rest,
no walking under ladders, gypsy's palm uncrossed,
mirror by the bed – this cobwebbed membrane, net

in which I swam, my mother kept
hidden in a drawer – *that's your luck,
you'll never drown.* Well, we were drowning then,

the threat we never quite believed, that she'd take off
leaving us to founder. We did our best.
We carried on, makeshift, from which I understood

there's luck and luck. I love the sea. I learned
to swim but even in the shallows I flounder,
never dare put my head underwater.

For brothers

which is close to *bothers;*
their love which is spoken of
though not always

by brothers. For as in arms,
in blood or law; for full and step
and half; for those of a certain age

for whom all friends are *bro;*
for those not brotherly at all; for *Joseph's,*
Abel's, Fifty-Fafty's; for my three grown
men, still thirteen, ten and five years old.

Fox count

Two tonight; one on our path just outside.
We heard the clang of the dustbin lid
and peered through the curtains,
saw him long-legged and thin. Your torch
picked out the white tip of his brush,
the glint of his eyes. The next was bright orange,
as thin, and scouring the patch of rough woodland
behind our garden. Cub season
makes them bold. Our friend says they've taken
most of her ducks. She'd finish
them if she could; just one shot is all it takes
if aimed right, but she wouldn't hunt.
She saw a fox once caught by the hounds,
a froth of hot pink spurting from it, *the blood*
boiled in the panicked run.
Others we've seen speeding over the road
in the dark or dodging into a neighbour's garden.
One stood at the gate as if taking the air.
After that it's just signs, bin bags torn
and scattered, a flash of eyes, dog fox's
yip yip, the vixen's pitched higher
calling her hunger into the night.

News

Whatever the truth of the breakneck
midnight ride that carried the news
to Aix from Ghent, or the other ride that spread
the alarm through Concord, Medford, Lexington

what stays in the head was the pace,
on a par with the flying legs
of the Shogun messengers, *Hikayaku* –
not pausing for rest, or sleep; not checked

by boundaries, like Mercury
speeding the dead to the underworld,
or the here-one-minute-gone-the-next
of the English sweat that sent the king

from bed to bed in a bid to outwit
the drenched mattress, rigours, chills;
which brings to mind the *lest we forget*
and the men lost to the fetid breath

of another fever. Then the threat that came next,
dismissed till the children died at their desks;
dismissed, the man who warned,
of the speed of its spread, so they carried on,

West End theatres, restaurants;
crowds come to cheer in Albert Square.
As for who was taken, who was left
or what was passed in the air, on the breath

and what was said, and said again:
some laid blame and some made shift
some of us heard, and some of us read
and turned the page, and some of us wept.

You aren't born yet

In China it's already your birthday.
I send you greetings in Pin Yin
before bed. You're *making breakfast*,
on my way to work; but in the hospital

it's two a.m. You aren't born yet.
Too soon, they said; *the wrong way round*.
You come before your face is ready,
without lashes or eyebrows

feet first, as if you can't wait
to touch earth. Since then
you've been pacing it, greedy
for the world. You wanted girls

and food and drugs, *to get away…*
until the black months came;
bad dreams, night sweats,
the dicky stomach. You slept

till there were no dreams left,
until the change in mood
that had us racing after you
as you careered from home to friend

to hospital, scattered clothes and tablets,
gave away your music, books,
threatened *abroad* . And when you left,
packing just the night before,

visa, passport, cash and medicine
pushed in with socks and water,
purifying tablets… *not ready*
was the one thought in my head.

You wake us now at four in the morning,
forgetting we're eight hours behind.
Shengri Kuaile, I say, although in China
they don't celebrate the same.

I say I'll make a cake and blow the candles
as you would, before they're all lit; don't say,
I know it's best you went, or how I've dreamt
about you every night since then –

a young man, schoolboy, baby
with that jaundiced look; the hospital
at two a.m. You're not yet born,
and in China it's already your birthday.

Nakasendo

Tiny against the mountain they struggle
to stay upright. Here is the black of a winter sky
peppered white. Each tree clinging
to rock carries its own fragile load
of snow that has fallen all day and will fall
all night. This is station twenty-nine
of the Nakasendo road. Five hundred feet
above sea level. Their boots and cloaks
are never warm enough. Flakes of snow
blur their eyelashes, ice spikes their cheeks.
Under the wide brims of their hats, the glint
of their eyes. It is so cold, so cold,
they can no longer feel their fingers or toes.

Winter song

This is your poem, our darling, our love,
our little one come in summer.
These are your words for the cold of the year,
ice underfoot, dark drawing near.
Here is your song for the flakes of white blown,
for the moon coming up, round as a bowl.

The kiss

When I ask she lifts her head, touches her nose
to mine, the way her Arabic grandma
has shown her. I love this delicacy.
It brings to mind the horses, two greys
in the field on our way home; how they run
into buffets of wind, their soft whicker
as they meet, proffer their cold noses
to each other. How they stand in the openness
of sky and bending grass, pale manes blown
across their necks. How attentive
to each other. And I hope that I can love her,
my granddaughter, with this same kindness
and economy, one touch to say everything;
love her also with a lift under the arms,
boisterous in the air, the way the horses swing
their shapely heads. And with delight
because she greets me with the same;
and passionate, the way I loved her mother;
but more because her mother's grown
and she's so small; and intimately,
courteous, nose to nose,
tender as speechless animals.

Notes

p35. **The blessing**: *shukran* – thank you; *anhar* – rivers; *binti* – girl; *la* – no

p37. **At Lovell Quinta**: Lovell Quinta is an arboretum in Cheshire created by Sir Bernard Lovell in the mid 1950s.

p41. **Fingula**: In Irish mythology one of the children of Lir changed into a swan given the gift of music by her stepmother. Fingula's brothers also changed into swans.

p42. **Fiachra**: Swans wings in flight are said to sound like singing.

p50. **Under the hill**: Standedge Tunnel is the longest, highest, deepest canal tunnel in England. Leggers 'walked' the barges through the tunnel with their feet against the tunnel roof.

p70. **Medlock**: In 1872 in Manchester the river Medlock flooded the cemetery at Philips Park. Graves were unearthed, coffins broken and bodies washed away, many of them never to be recovered.

p74. **Hide**: John Atkinson Grimshaw was a Victorian artist best known for his urban scenes.

p78. **For brothers**: *Fifty-Fafty's* is a story by Robert Westall in which a long-lost brother is murdered by his siblings.

p80. **News**: The man who warned of the speed of the spread of the 1918 Spanish flu outbreak was Manchester medical officer James Niven.

p81. **You aren't born yet**: Hanyu Pinyin is the official romanisation system for standard Mandarin Chinese. *Shengri Kuaile* – Happy Birthday

p83. **Nakasendo**: Nakasendo is an ancient Japanese trail depicted in prints by Hiroshige.

Milton Keynes UK
Ingram Content Group UK Ltd.
UKHW011103010424
440421UK00005B/477

9 781738 405916